Copyright © 2019 Tekkan
Artwork Copyright © 2019

All rights reserved.
First Printing, 2019
ISBN 978-1-7343510-3-3

To contact Tekkan please email:
buddhaboy1289@gmail.com

This book is dedicated to Mike Finley,
King of the St. Paul poets.

How to Read My Poems

I am an ordinary guy living a middle class life. I may imagine what it would be like to put on a wingsuit and jump off a mountain, but my stock-in-trade is the exploration of "everyday mind." I look for transcendent meaning in the ordinary happenings of daily life. I write in the morning everyday, and try to distill experience down to essentials. It is easy to overlook the instant-by-instant process of seeing, thinking, and responding to life — but in reality that is what life is.

The mind is self-interested and driven by powerful emotions. I look around and determine what to do. I judge what's worthy, and establish a list of priorities. My likes and dislikes become signposts, and if I am not careful I find myself repeating a pattern of behavior, and get stuck, narrowly seeing, feeling, experiencing — and then where is novelty?

Spring has sprung but today is chilly. I love watching the seasons change in a succession of little details, because the seasons are so much bigger than what's going on in my mind. There is always a lot going on in nature, and my practice is to open, so that more of reality may penetrate my consciousness.

I practice opening my awareness to the world inside and outside of me. Consciousness is a miracle — but I have to learn how to use the gift of Consciousness. This is what my poetry is about.

My daughter, Jocelyn MacDonald, is a wonderful artist. Her art work graces this book.

I am Barry MacDonald. I received the *dharma* name, *Tekkan*, which means, Iron Man, a settled practitioner of great determination.

— *Tekkan*

Everyday Mind XIII

We turn our clocks
an hour backwards
on November 3rd
but regardless
the darkness lengthens.

Compassion was boring he said and if
People would leave him alone everything
Would be o-ke-do-ke but if someone
Were so careless as to cross his path as

If they were a delinquent slinky
At the top of a flight of steps he would
Topple them over and gleefully watch them
Tumble down the stairs — but that was many

Years ago — before he found a seat with
The circles of sober alcoholics
And now he displays a generous and
Warm curmudgeoncy and he practices

A sharp and antiseptic honesty
Finagling somehow to become happy.

He is grateful
sobriety allows
him to enjoy his
grandchildren.

A mist is occupying Stillwater
This morning obscuring the homes and trees
While clearing a little in these minutes
With outlines becoming visible

As it seems an overbearing winter
Sky is descending from its lofty height
Settling on the earth as a moist layer
Of overnight snow is melting on the

Grass making it easy to believe that
There are no separate things and events
As the not quite freezing air and sky are
Saturating my consciousness with the

Expectation of much colder days and
The satisfaction of being prepared.

The snow is melting
on the metal of the
shovel as I'm moving
my legs and scraping
the driveway.

The sky is snow white again this morning
As white as yesterday although today
It has resumed its accustomed height and
The trees are making a leafless and a

Tangled outline underneath the looming
Sky as the air is warmer and the snow
Has vanished as if it were only a
Fantasy while the grass and the bushes

Are sprinkled with drops of water as all
The winters I remember are hinting
That these predominately cloudy days
Are here for the duration almost as

If a lid were slipped over the earth and
A covering will remain until spring.

The details
are predictable
yet somehow they
surprise.

Our group was removing the cushions from
The chapel and returning them to the
Cabinet down the corridor as we
Were chatting happily as usual

After meditation with everyone
Putting away the bells and the altar
And returning the chairs to their places
Inside the chapel amidst the hubbub

Of happy bantering conversation
Mixing activity with blather as
I was trimming the candle that needed an
Expenditure of effort because it's

Been neglected with me pulling the knife
Towards me while my thinking was aflutter.

Slicing my knuckle
open reminded me
of the simplicity of
doing one thing
at a time.

My instructions on driving motorbikes
Informed me not to fixate on potholes
Because doing so would guarantee my
Hitting the pothole because the bike goes

Exactly where I'm looking so I learned
To cast my sight strategically to lean
Into a curve and most of all to be
Alert but these days I'm writing about

Politics and following the news and
Watching deceitful personalities
And fabricated incendiary
Narratives and even if I'm alert

It's hard to absorb the psychodrama
Without becoming somewhat cynical.

Wearing a helmet
while reading news
isn't helpful.

I use an electric clipper only
To trim the pesky hair that sprouts under
My nostrils because the razor is quite
Impossible to maneuver there and

I hate looking in the mirror on the
Inside of the sun visor of my car
And seeing several egregious bristles
But sometimes when I push the switch to start

The clipper nothing happens and swearing
Doesn't help so I drop the clipper on
The countertop repeatedly until
For some mysterious reason it works —

It's absolutely necessary to
Jar the clipper so much to make it start.

I'm not sure
refinement
is a fair
description
of my life.

I get invested emotionally
In what I write and after polishing
A poem I print and place it inside
A briefcase and leave it until evening

And the lapse of hours occupied with
Other activity separates me
From my jewel so when reading it again
Sometimes I gain the clarity to see

Egregious errors but when the time comes
To edit a hundred poems at once
Initially I'm repulsed and ashamed
Because reading them is like looking in

A mirror and becoming engrossed with
My mannerisms stripped of delusions.

I need to persevere
to reconnect with
the original
inspiration.

Zen masters will question — who are you — and
Offering your name or profession or
Your status within society aren't
The answers to satisfy them as they

Will ask who is looking through your eyes what was
Your original face your face before
Conception what is the true color of
Your heart why is your hand so much like the

Buddha's hand and they will assert that you
Do not exist and you cannot seize the
Answers by anything you do or by
Anything you don't do while your thinking

Isn't helpful and not thinking isn't
Much better because you can't stop thinking.

A *hintergeanken*
is a suspicion
of something
that can't be
admitted.

We have had our baptismal snowfall of
The season and as is typical of
The beginning when the temperature
Hovers about freezing the snow was wet

And heavy and the morning afterwards
The sticky snow is adhering to the
Trunks and the bare branches of the trees and
Giving to Stillwater a fantasy

Frosted candy land appearance but the
Chill of the snow is sobering the white
Sky is ominous and the chunky piles
Of snow the city plows have left along

The street are reminding me of twenty
Years of dragging winter experience.

Atop the asphalt
of my driveway
the thinnest layer of
ice demarks where
the rain became the snow.

We gather within the spacious and
Windowed atrium of a church we one
Hundred sixty sober alcoholics
As we do every year celebrating

Our sobriety on Thanks Giving Day
Each of us taking a turn saying our
Names and briefly reciting why we are
Grateful while everyone is listening

And it's always a happy occasion
Greeting companions again we haven't
Seen for a year reacquainting ourselves
Enjoying conversation preceding

And following our seated statements as
The room reverberates with our chatter.

Imagine the havoc
one hundred sixty
active drug addicts
and alcoholics
would be.

While I was visiting a temple in
Japan focusing myself with intense
Meditation newspapers would publish
Artwork presenting images of grass

Or of tulips and within the tulips
Or the grass outlines of a duck or of
A cat would be concealed but to see the
Duck or the cat I would have to squint my

Eyes just so as the optical trick was
Finagled with tiny dots upon a
Cheap quality of paper and sometimes
I could see the duck within the tulips

And sometimes I couldn't so I wondered
Is this another way of doing Zen?

A grim and
experienced monk
wasn't amused
by my question.

Soggy snow will make a slushy noise if
You toss a shovelful in the air and
Listen to it settle on a pile but
I don't spare the time for frivolity

When clearing driveways as it's too much work
And the snow blower is useless getting
Clogged as it does so I stab the shovel
Into the snow and onto the asphalt

And become a plow by keeping my legs
Moving pushing and pushing and pushing
And I'm bundled for the exercise with
Only two points of weakness which are my

Thumbs even when it's not too cold because
Even in mittens they are outstanding.

My toes are snug
inside my moonboots
but thumbs are
vulnerable to the
burning cold.

They hardly seem like anything falling
Constantly all morning and into the
Afternoon as the tiniest snowflakes
Steadily dropping from beyond the bare

Branches falling from a white sky distant
But impossible to gage the distance
Because there's nothing to compare it with
Beyond the bare branches only seeing

The white sky is inseparable from
The descent of the puniest of the
White snowflakes accumulating in the
Morning and throughout the afternoon and

Once I cleared the driveway and saw the black
Of the asphalt but now it's overcome.

White sky
and snowflakes
are sticking to
the bare branches.

In the dark hours before dawn sometimes I
Wake and then my thinking refuses to
Sleep and so there is the choice of whether
To lie in bed and passively review

My difficulties or to rise and dress
And sit before a computer screen with
My fingers poised and tapping out my thoughts
As they arise even though there's nothing

Special to discover and the thinking
Shapes itself around how the words will
Fit together and whether a flow of
Ideas and rhythm emerges and

Maybe a pursuit of something worthy
Of the effort of expression will come.

It's often a race
whether I reach a
destination before
dawn or I'm overcome
with drowsiness.

Stillwater

Regardless of the weather my comings
And goings lead me almost every day
To a view of the broad river with its
Valley southwards while the sun is rising

And I also see the ornate mansions
Built during the era of the lumber
Barons with the harvested timber of
The time located atop the bluffs of

The city — usually I hurry
On my way but when the sun is shining
Reflecting off the river and glinting from
The windows of the mansions on the bluffs

I'm struck by the beauty of Stillwater —
The limestone the valley and the river.

The Crossing Bridge
three miles away
a mile across
gracefully spans
the distance.

The refraction of yellow and blue and
White that I see when looking downriver
At the sunlight on the water and the
Snowy banks of the valley are waves of

Light bouncing off the river and valley
And into my eyes where electrical
Impulses are creating a spectrum
Of color in gradients of detail

And when my friend says — isn't this morning
Beautiful — waves of sound are entering
My ears and creating a question and
Prompting an instantaneous response —

Yes it really is a beautiful day
After so many gloomy snowy days.

My head is
awash in
cosmic waves
creating
emotions.

If only I had a formidable
Horn protruding from the center of my
Forehead I would be presenting a most
Imposing appearance as a force to

Be wary of and of course it wouldn't
Do to support a warrior's armament
With a slack jawed slope-shouldered comportment —
I'd have to have a barrel chest and stout

Legs well apart and firmly placed upon
The earth and I would have to assume an
Uncompromising and a humorless
Attitude without sensitivity

Or subtlety because otherwise what
Would be the point of possessing the horn?

Who ever
heard of a
fastidious
or simpering
rhinoceros?

Only by looking in a mirror can
I assess the features of my face and
Thereby compare myself with others to
Play the game of identity based on

Comeliness or the lack of comeliness
And it seems so simple not to play the
Game — don't look and don't care — but not caring
Is hard to do while even a mirror

Is limited as it cannot reveal
To me the inside of my head behind
My eyes — how does the inside of my head
Look — is there something or nothing there to

See and yet my eyesight captures so much
Of the evanescing panorama.

There is no mirror
between the world and
me except the image of
me I interpose.

Rohatsu

Pain in the legs and back is expected
When doing repeated periods of
Meditation and it's continuous
And coincident with the arising

Of energy and it takes vigorous
Effort to stay in the lotus posture
Though the night of starting and ending bells
Seeing in the dim electric light the

Shadow of my unmoving seated form
Extending before me on the carpet —
The slow and careful placing of our feet
As we pace the minutes out in silence

Walking in a circle as we do does
Relieve the intensity of sitting.

Burning
like a
candle
through the
night.

The familiar neighborhood is transformed
By the descending snowflakes as I can
See the homes the bare trees the spiky pines
Obscurely through the snow as the specks of

Falling whiteness are everywhere as I
Left my car in the garage thinking it's
Better not to worry about getting
Stuck within the accumulation on

The streets walking to the office in my
Boots holding a thermos of coffee in
Each mitten I trudge along wondering
How can the sky be distinguished from the

Snow and realizing the snow a while
Ago was a swelling and rolling ocean.

Tiny flakes
touch my
face and
inform
me of
the cold.

If I were to remark there is no time
And that there isn't any distance and
Also that there aren't separate events
You may think that I am nonsensical

But in nature seconds and minutes and
Hours do not exist apart from human
Fabrication and the idea of
Infinity is a phantom of the

Mind — also I cannot pick up an inch
From the ground and the miles I amble in
Summer from my home to the Crossing Bridge
Over the river and back to my home

On the north hill is just manner of
Measuring what I can do with my feet.

The swelling ocean
evaporating water
drifting clouds
and snow are
continuous.

When it's cold outside I use a trick to
Make things easier by opening the
Outside door and inserting the key while
Standing in the warmth inside the home so

I don't have to stand outside fumbling
With my bare hands in the cold because my
Mittens are too thick to be able to
Handle locking the door and of course I

Dress in layers of clothes as if I were
Weaving a chrysalis about me and
It's a pleasurable moment in the
Day when getting out of bed that I can

Insert my barest feet into the most
Luxurious and fuzziest of socks.

The foundation of
the coldest of days
is a warm and
comfy pair of
socks.

Holiday Poem

If I were much more weighty than I am
It would be fun lumbering into a
Room and striding slowly without any
Wiggly toes and swishing my meager

Tail and flapping my exorbitant ears
Using my demeanor to demonstrate
My excitement and my intention to
Exact a moment of retribution

And I might even pause for a while to
Allow my enormous presence in the
Tiny room to exert authority
And then I would trumpet my voice about

And then with intensity of purpose
I would seize on the rascal with my trunk.

I would use my
elephant's weight
to sit upon and
squash the pesky
relative.

I make an effort not to be fooled by
Events into believing that I am
Unworthy when I am discouraged or
That I am superior when things are

Going well because I think the cosmos
Is an unceasing emanation of
Waves more than light and sound but also my
Perceptions and responses come in waves

And I cannot wrench myself into a
Happy undulation when in a trough
And I'm making an effort to recall
There cannot be a crest without a trough —

To be a floating jellyfish or a
Masterful surfer — that is the question.

A reactive
and resentful
jellyfish doesn't
recognize
waves.

Poor Henry who has kidney disease is
Looking up at me from the floor with
A steady gaze intending I think to
Express something but it's hard knowing what

He wants as he's been fed and I'm happy
To observe that he's been eating almost
Normally although in quite small portions
And when he's looking at me in this way

It usually does mean he's hungry so
I do feed him because the disease will
Make him constipated which causes him
Not to eat so when he wants to eat I

Seize the opportunity to give him
The food he needs to live a little more.

Henry is a cat
with a penetrating
gaze but I don't know
what he's trying to say.

Henry makes a raspy disgruntled growl
Johnnie whines incessantly for his food
Kitcat is an adolescent fool who
Takes a rascal's pleasure in wrestling

And biting the smaller cats about their
Necks and Kitcat pushes items off the
Kitchen counter seizing my attention
But I am dominating by turning

Doorknobs and opening the tins of food —
Sometimes I am serious with Kitcat
Staring at him with dissatisfaction
Pronouncing nonsensical noises and

Looming over him and raising a hand
While he rolls on his back wanting to play.

I go about the
house singing to
the cats and they
don't take me
seriously.

Humans are funny animals who can
Acquire a supplementary skin
Through cleverness and selection and I
Fashion for myself a layer of warmth

And comfort in the winter by wearing
Garments composed of synthetic fiber
Called polar fleeces countering the drab
Landscape consisting of longer nights and

Frozen air and the perpetual brown
Of the trees and the white of the snow I
Am wearing the brightest orange and red
And green and the bluest blue bell of blue

And my vulnerable wiggly toes
Are swaddled in the warmest fuzzy socks.

Cat hair sticks to
the polar fleeces
and I find myself
perpetually
picking off the hairs.

People may suppose that managing a
Political movement is all about
Promoting a system of ideals
But in modern America the trick

Consists in persuading mass numbers of
Voters to hate the right sort of people
As the whole operation depends on
Directing attention away from the

Mismanagement and the thievery that
Politicos are engaged in because
The American middle class always
Produces the most stupendous pile of

Taxpayer's money in the history
Of the world and the money is the prize.

Great white sharks constantly
swim to prevent drowning —
politicos accuse others
of doing what they
do.

I listen to politicos and know
They can't possibility believe what they are
Saying and they overlook the fact that
Their words are on video and when at

Different times because of altering
Circumstances they take exactly the
Opposite sides of the same issue — all
The while professing utter sincerity —

They seem unconcerned that such audacious
Shameless hypocrisy is obvious
To anyone paying attention but
They rely on the ignorance and the

Fickleness of public opinion and
On a sympathetic media.

They are brazen
because of the
overabundance
of anger and
ignorance.

There are blue skies in every season but
When the snow is accumulated on
The ground and when the air is freezing then
As the sun rises on the horizon

And illuminates the river valley
The sun is a glowing brilliant disk of
Orange lighting the graceful cables of
The Crossing Bridge in the distance and

Shining everywhere on the snow on the
Ground and I can see the sparkle of the
Sun refracted in the pinpoint jewels of
Blue and green and red appearing as if

The snow were a magical blanket and
Winter is worthy of celebration.

So often during winter
it seems as though
an overcast lid were
stretched over the sky.

Words as I compose them on a screen by
Paying attention to their rhythms and
Sounds and meanings by training myself to
Seize on whatever is piquant today —

Believing as I do there is always
Something worthy of celebration in
A day — allow me to forget about
My troubles for an hour and the hunt for

And discovery of the perfect fit for
The exact word is so pleasurable
That satisfaction suffuses my days
And difficulties that would otherwise

Sap my energy and discourage me
Will seem no more than a passing trifle.

The act of
spontaneously
choosing
a word
is joyous.

However do the trees survive through the
Winter when the ground is frozen and their
Roots are inert and the tips of their twigs
Are leafless and all they can do is to

Stand in the wind and create a howling —
And however does my heart beat itself
And my lungs breathe themselves as if they were
Disconnected from whatever concern

Is presently occupying my mind —
And are these happenings similar to
Or the same as the energy causing
The sun to burn itself — and the stars of

The Milky Way to burn themselves as they
Are revolving around a massive hole?

The thinnest of clouds
are moving across
the sky unhindered
by any thought of
needing to perform.

I am resolving today to dispose
Of the things that are cluttering my life
As just a glance around my office desk
Reveals the many business cards that I

Have no memory of collecting and
There is the Christmas card from a person
I barely knew who died years ago and
Perhaps I decided to keep the card

Because he was an artist and sent a
Drawing of Dayton Ohio where he
Lived showing the skyline of the city
Maybe on a sunny afternoon when

He traced his city in graceful lines and
Now I am reluctant to part with it.

There is a tug
to hang on to
little parcels of
memory.

I am a natural meditator
As the sand in the desert is too hot
To swivel within during the day and
Inactivity conserves energy

For my hunting in the night when the grains
Of the sand are cooled and continuous
Motion is easier than thinking and
Sashaying and waiting and flicking my

Tongue are exciting as I determine
Where to go depending on which of the
Forks of my tongue will taste the tang of a
Scent for undulation and waiting and

Flicking and watching and coiling about
For an impulsive application of fangs.

Vibrating
fear
anger
danger
makes
me
rattle.

Living alone for the first time during
Christmas and New Year's Day for me is a
Different rhythm as the house needs a
Cleaning and in the process of wiping

Dust off the piano and of throwing
Out containers of unused food and of
Scrubbing every surface and corner of
The refrigerator while listening

To music I am quite surprisingly
Generating enthusiasm while
Accidentally I nudge the cuckoo
Clock and hear the familiar ticking

I haven't heard for many years as the
House is beginning to be a home again.

The clock was
dusty and idle
because my ex-wife
disliked the
cuckooing.

When working for the Andersen Windows
Corporation Jim merged his body with
The mechanical repetition of
Assembling windows for a number

Of hours a day but in retirement
He gives his attention to the sky and
The trees to rivers and lakes in a hunt
For the miraculous revelation

Of birds — he told me why the house sparrows
Were brought from England and released into
The parks of New York City — to eat the
Moth larvae ravaging the trees and now

The sparrows have spread everywhere killing
The butterflies native birds and flowers.

Jim sees the wood ducks
blue-winged teals
trumpeter swans
prairie warblers
painted redstarts.

I don't know the differences between a
Finch and a yellow-bellied sapsucker
And the only bird I see every day
Is a bird requiring no special

Knowledge or talent to identify —
The somber crow impervious to the
Hardships of winter — but Jim possesses
The sensibility to admire the

Variety and elegance of birds
And by virtue of his passion insight
Animates him and the air and the trees
The river valley and Stillwater's bluffs

Are full of evanescent loveliness
On the fly and seen only in moments.

What a gift it is
to be on the hunt
searching the air
for just a glimpse
of beauty.

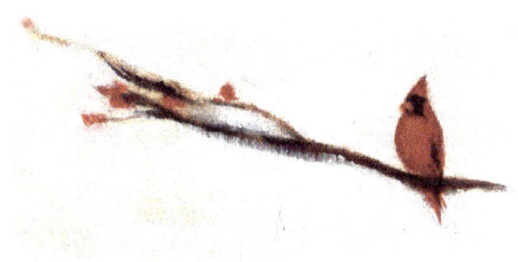

I remember an hour before dawn
In Kyoto thirty years ago that
Was such a lovely departure from the
Consistently sweltering summer air

When the window was open and rain was
Pattering on a walkway outside and
I can hear the sound of the rain again
Recall the luscious coolness of the air

When I wrapped myself within a blanket
Savoring swaddling warmth in the dark
While the bamboo was knocking together
And rain was spattering on the concrete —

Whatever worries I carried then are
Forgotten but I remember the rain.

I remember the
throbbing of cicadas
through a summer haze
while looking over Kyoto
from the eastward mountains.

Why do I remember some things and not
Others and who does the remembering
Because I'm not quite the assemblage
Of propensities that I was and yet

Some experience is echoing through
The decades as I have applied myself
To accumulate a compendium
Of knowledge and skills and usually

In circumstances my actions are a
Repetition of my past behavior
And I don't think much about responding
But in conversation with family

Sometimes I discover we have said things
Or been to places I have forgotten.

Perhaps I'm like a
whirlpool in a river
swirling and forgetting
as much as remembering.

It doesn't matter whether I'm in the
Mood to write because when I arrive at
My desk while the sun is rising I am
Alert and able to leverage my

Thinking and whether the rippling of
My mind is rehearsing the reasons why
I should be angry or I am blaming
People because I'm lonely and they don't

Care or whether I'm happy and the sun
Is resplendent — it doesn't matter if
I'm moody — because I love weighing the
Meaning of words and searching for just the

Right angle to communicate with you
And whatever I was feeling is gone.

Please understand
my poems employ
turning words which
emanate
satisfaction.

Christmas is done — New Year's Eve is coming —
Soon the seasonal landmarks will have passed
And I have a habit of taking out
My binoculars and seeing onto

Spring on the far horizon where lilac
Bushes and cherry and apple trees are
Blossoming but between here and there is
A long weary trudge through the tundra of

Winter and I know from experience
That into March and April and even
May there are teasing intervals when it
Seems that winter is finally finished

And yet an arctic front descends on us
With abominable wet heavy snow.

It's better to
put the binoculars
away and appreciate
that every snowflake is
unique.

I am the only person in my home
With the ability to open doors
And tins of food while I am surrounded
By personalities mischievous

Whiny and grumpy — when I'd like to sleep
Just a little longer in the morning
There's a pounding on my door summoning
Me to the kitchen to open the tins

Of food — though I've become proficient at
Ignoring noises — and whenever I
Am at home I can depend on my cats
For the fellowship a lonely guy needs —

They don't impose themselves excessively
They are less temperamental than people.

Henry is wasting away
with kidney disease and
at some point I'll need
to determine when
to put him under.

We had a conversation this morning
On the occasion of New Year's Day and
We sober alcoholics discussed the
Endeavor of living free from the snares

Of unkind thoughts and bitterness and free
Of every fear of the future and we
Would like to be liberated from our
Gloom despondency and disappointments

Because you see in our isolation
The world appears as a hall of funhouse
Mirrors showing a repetition of
Distorted images but when talking

To each other the hall of mirrors is
Dissolved and we see the world as it is.

Companionship and
communication
break down barriers
and we find ourselves
liberated.

I love the attention that comes to me
When I am able to express myself
And be understood — I love having the
Company of a companion able

To express her experience of the
Ephemeral world from a point of view
I could never have come to on my own
Because I am a drop of consciousness

Within an ocean of consciousness and
By myself I am incomplete tending
To dark meditations and I don't need
An affirmation of my opinions

I just love an exploration of our
Differing and complimentary views.

The unborn
undying
world is
beyond
knowing.

I am inclined to be apart from group
Opinion while not being overtly so
Because I recognize the power of
Mass hypnosis and sometimes I do doubt

Whether my view is accurate so I
Watch and play to my strength consisting
Of an underlying intuition
Despite the presence of ubiquitous

Controversy and chaos that things are
OK as they are determining me
To do what I can to be active and
Kind and optimistic with the people

I meet because my sphere of influence
Surpasses the extent of my knowledge.

This is an unceasing
and wounding cosmos
compelling me to
seek healing and
strength.

I brushed his hair for a final time and
Picked him up facing him to Johnnie and
Kitcat urging them to say goodbye and
To avoid inducing stress I put him

Into the carrier backwards so he
Couldn't see what I was doing until
He was inside — he was free to sniff and
Wander about the room until the vet

Removed him for a few minutes so she
Could insert the catheters into his
Veins — I held him in my lap — the vet pushed
The plungers of the syringes — pumped the

Drugs inside of him and so suddenly
He collapsed in my hands and departed.

Henry was a white cat
with orange spots and the
tips of ears were frozen
off in a winter before
he was recued years ago.

They were not large enough to wield a
Rifle or to thrust a bayonet in
Anger but the teenage drummer boys of
The Civil War communicated the

Commands of generals amidst the noise
Of battle with dozens of cadences
Signaling when to rally where to meet
When to attack and retreat — and they served

In field hospitals — but when the dispersed
Drummers on the field initiated
The steady beating of the long roll the
Soldiers were summoned in serried ranks

To master a terrible contest of
Minnie balls cannon balls and bayonets.

Drummers beat the
single and double drags
double stroke roll
flamadiddles
paradiddles
ratamacues
flam accents
flamacues
sextuplets
and ruffs.

On a clear morning in January
With snow on the ground and a chill in the
Wind my cottonwood is bathed in the light
Of the rising sun and the multitude

Of its limbs and twigs the entirety
Of its unsymmetrical sprouting so
High into the air is revealed in
The orange light of a rising sun in

Winter — every deep groove of its bark and
The remotest twig at the end of a
Crooked branch is visible and apart
From any abstract notion I conceive

Of what constitutes beauty as its quiet
Slumbering transcends my valuations.

On the corner of my
property by the fire
hydrant it is standing
appearing in all its
unexplainable presence.

It's easy to adopt a pattern of
Behavior repeatedly every day
Not noticing the ephemeral turn
Of events but I am seeing the sun

Rising on a couple of days in a clear
Sky over the drab landscape of winter
With a brilliant orange light and I am
Noticing the slanting of the sunrise

Lighting trees in the neighborhood for just
Several minutes of the day when the
Trees are reflecting the same resplendent
Orange as the sun while the houses and

The streets are not — as the sun caresses
The trees for a moment and passes on.

The chill of winter
reaches even inside
a heated home and
warm socks are a
necessity.

My alarm rings at 4:40 a.m.
And usually I'm able to leave
My bed and take care of my three felines —
Until last week — every morning my cats

Anticipate me watching and waiting
To be brushed and fed as I launch into
Nonsensical banter and song because
Whatever my cats derive from me has

Nothing to do with the meaning of words
But the joy and enthusiasm I
Generate does communicate and my
Little friends appreciate rituals

I believe as I learn an important
Lesson — I don't have to be serious.

Now that Henry's passed away
I'm discovering an
extra 10 minutes of
free time but I'd
rather have Henry.

My cats do not pretend to be happy
When they are obstinately annoyed
And I can grab Kitcat by the scruff of
His neck or knead the fur of his forehead

With my fingers or toss him on his back
And aggressively tickle his tummy
And he demonstrates his enjoyment by
Pursuing me after I walk away —

His intentions are clear when he's whining
For his food which is a habit he learned
From Johnnie — but people may be smiling
With their eyes and face while truly they are

Differing bored and not listening and
I might as well be talking to a wall.

Generally I am
optimistic and
enthusiastic but
it's hard for me to
smile for a photo.

I'm in a predicament because I
Know I need to be happy in photos
But the more determined I become to
Smile the more difficulty I'm having —

People are urging me to summon a
Lighthearted memory and a joyful
Expression will naturally blossom —
I don't doubt the effectiveness of the

Suggestion — I am sure it works for them —
They have pushed me in a good direction
And I'm resolved to follow their advice
But presently the harder I try the

Less likely I am to smile so perhaps
For now I will be happy with a grin.

Being
perfectly
purposely
spontaneous is
tricky.

It hasn't snowed for a week and the snow
On the ground is crusty on top and though
There isn't much wind when the slightest whiff
Touches the exposed skin on my face as

I'm moving from my car to the coffee
Shop I'm alerted instantly it is
Cold — I remember seeing the first drops
Of a summer rain striking the concrete

Before me on a Saturday in June
Thinking these are very large raindrops — then
I was plunked on my forehead — but today
It's necessary to be wary of

The ice on the walkway as a moment's
Inattention could result in a fall.

As I'm walking the
folds of my jeans are
communicating
the biting cold of
January.

The cold lingers upon the skin after
Entering a heated home for moments
Reminding me of what the cold is as
Nothing else could do and then I hear the

Whoosh of the furnace and the hum of the
Aquarium and the printer and I
Close my eyes listening allowing my
Ears to absorb the waves of sound throbbing

Within the room and there is the pulsing
Of my blood and the beating of my heart
But try as I might I can't do without
My eyes and outside the window beyond

A fringe of bare branches a thin layer
Of clouds very high up is hovering.

Bare awareness
is so much more
peaceful than the
fretful hassle of
thinking.

Our conversations have had an impact
As I've had the opportunity to
Hear about your experience and
Concerns and to see with your vision how

The world is manifesting — I'm trying
To decipher the explicit and the
Unspoken messages we have exchanged —
I'm attending to a tide within me

Attempting to surf my emotions and
Aspiring to poise and nimbleness
Knowing that I need to be in the flow
Surrendering expectations aiming

To be as light as a feather with you
And allowing the waves to carry me.

I'll paddle my
surfboard out
anticipating.

There are some movies that I love to watch
Because I am enchanted with the play
Of emotions on display — I like the
Antagonism of an oppressive

Society with stylish mendacity
When devils are perversely attractive —
The dynamic of rebellion against
Overwhelming odds overburdens a

Woman and a man creating a sense
Of mission compelling sacrifice and
Courage and every tremulous motion
Of their faces touches indecision and

Resolve — scorn and hatred — apprehension
And love — and the emotions resonate.

But when actors
venture political
opinions on current
issues their sanctimony
reverberates.

I know better than to come to my desk
With the intention of writing while my
Thinking is persistently distracted
And the effort assumes the aspect of

A tug of war with part of me striving
To enunciate ethereal words
While the rest of me is occupied with
Visceral urges as yesterday I

Signed up with a dating site and composed
A profile and uploaded my photos
And now I can't seem to keep myself from
Grasping for my phone anticipating

A bouncing bodacious and beautiful
Woman with a blossoming of welcome.

Whatever
ethereal words
might have come
are entirely
consumed.

To be alone with my thoughts and have no
Other perspective to balance mine would
Be an impoverishment of spirit
Because companionship far surpasses

The intellect as we communicate
So much of affection and harmony
With an attitude and gesture of the
Body in unguarded moments even

The slightest emotion flickers between
Us through our eyes and faces transforming
A tedious afternoon into an
Oasis that doesn't depend upon

Opinion but does bespeak a happy
Exploration of what life could become.

Difference is a
spice of intriguing
possibility.

It's almost a shame to sprinkle letters
And words across the pristine whiteness of
A page but if I didn't how could my
Playful exploration ever emerge —

I imagine emptiness to be black
With nothing inside of it and the black
Letters sprawling in serried lines upon
A page could be a frightful tickling

But the lovely and shapely appearance
Of my letters skipping along the page
May serve as a brave assertion of my
Frolic in the face of oblivion

But how could emptiness be black or white
And how does life and color emanate?

A bare tree under
a white sky in
January is a wilder
version of my
poem.

It is easy to become lost in thought
Thinking it's important to grasp the right
Ideology and the correct point
Of view but it is an inspiration

To ponder what was my original
Face and who was I before being born —
Am I more akin to the line of the
Horizon in the distance? To the clouds

Drifting in the sky? To the up-thrusting
Of a mountain weathering and slowly
Eroding? While it's true I do possess
Ideas and ideas do possess

Me doesn't being encompass so much
More than the categories of a mind?

Am I also the
burning sphere
of rock becoming
the earth with
breathable air?

I'll send a text and leave a message on
Your machine doing my business for the
Morning while waiting for a response and
Checking my phone in my pocket again

Anticipating your voice desiring
A connection imagining what you
May sound like as we haven't spoken yet
But there are the words we've exchanged and I

Have your profile on the website as you've
Brought me along setting the time and day
For our meeting asking me to choose the
Locale and I asserted Quixotic

Coffee yesterday and tomorrow is
Coming quickly but you haven't said yes.

Your figure is so
curvy in places
stimulating me
to extend myself
anticipating.

At about 4 a.m. if I leave my door
Open Johnnie comes in and begins to
Gnaw on a leg of the marble top stand
With his teeth because he knows doing that

Bothers me and I will say — stop it — and
When he keeps gnawing I will rise from bed
And toss him out of the room and close the
Door — then Kitcat pounces on Johnnie

Overwhelming him and then Johnnie yowls
And I rise from bed again and open
The door saying — shush — which they do for a
While but then the ruckus starts again while

I am determined not to get up so
Early but it's impossible to sleep.

My cats are determined that
I should feed them
at 4 a.m. — but I
won't — not until
4:40.

Even though it's not written into our
Laws and people do their business without
Being aware of its power it's hard
To deny the contention between us

Of a hierarchy of dominance
Whereby we sort ourselves in levels of
Status and influence involving the
Recognition of a thousand telltale

Signals of beauty intelligence and
Ability and I need to give
Biology respect but I rely
For comfort on spiritual jujitsu —

If I can be playful in my thinking
I will have the companionship I need.

There is enough
novelty and love
to go around.

From day to day it's easy to forget
The line of the horizon in the distance
Is moving at a thousand miles an hour
As the earth is spinning on its axis

And today the sky is solidly white
And all the trees are coated with fresh snow
And the air is interspersed with large flakes
Swirling separately and slowly down

And I realize on this chilly day
In January when the morning is
Marvelous that the sun is resplendent
As it's moving overhead and all that

I am seeing is a reflection of
The penetrating and life-giving light.

Have you not noticed
that this place where
we are living is
exceedingly odd?

It's problematic being me in the
Cold walking outside to and from my car
While managing keys and holding the two
Thermoses of coffee that I need to

Be human and on occasion the load
Is increased with a bag of gym clothes and
A briefcase with the thermoses fitting
Under the crook of an elbow with the

Handles of the bag looping through an arm
But while wearing mittens my fingers are
Mostly useless and then locking my door
And lifting the door of the garage is

An ordeal but I suppose that's just what
Happens when living in Minnesota.

I could always make
two trips back and
forth but that's too
much work.

A girl informed me of Saturday night
Contra dancing where I could always find
A partner and at the same time sashay
And promenade and do a cute little

Turn that is called the do si do with a
Succession of various women of
Different comportment and sizes and
Ages which I enjoy very much and

I would like to go back every week but
When summoned to — swing your girl — I got so
Dizzy and stayed dizzy with visions of
A surging ocean of women whirling

About me that I became light-headed
And had to sit down to regain balance.

I haven't felt so
dizzy since I was
a high school student
chewing tobacco for
the first time.

The oval I am making of my palms
And of my fingers as they are lying
In my lap as my arms are relaxing on
My thighs as I am expressing the

Lotus position and meditating
Before leaving home — the oval of my
Hands are gently focusing my thoughts as
They are arising and passing as I

Am weighing the emotion tinged with every
Thought and discovering whether I am
Adverse attracted or neutral about
A thought and the most helpful part of my

Practice is not to cling to any thought
But learning to let go of every thought.

The uncluttered mind
is like a ball bouncing
down a mountain
stream
unhindered.

I wonder whether it's tiresome to
Read so many of my poems about
Sunrises while noticing my neglect
Of sunsets which are equally lovely

But sunrises are an inspiration
To me while a setting sun is weirdly
Disorienting and disquieting
As the light is vanishing revealing

The preponderance of a void sprinkled
About with pinpoints of starlight teasing
Me with questions and yearnings I have no
Way of satisfying — the questions are

A visceral trembling of spirit
And the yearning is for reassurance.

I just believe there
is something about the
balancing of day and
night hinting of the
imperishable.

When I am quiet enough there is the
Reverberation of my heart and the
Pulsation of my blood in my veins to
Accompany me and for the moment I

Don't have to think about the series of
Chores that weighs on my mind today and the
Challenge of performing a task and of
Satisfying the expectations of

My colleagues and of myself and for
The moment there is the simple pleasure
Of being apart from achievement and
Disappointment and then I recognize

There is a sanctuary within me
Apart from the clamor of my doings.

And then the sustenance
of mind and body
takes over and I move
doing
business.

He has never accepted his brushing
Like the others keeping aloof at a
Distance watching and knowing when I was
Through with them that I would come and stretch him

Before me facing him away from me
As I stroked him with the Furminator
Which is a sturdy brush with metal teeth
As every so often he'd turn and hiss

At me asserting his denial of
My diminution of his dominance
But over the years he's gotten playful
Turning on his back and grasping at the

Brush with his paws and kicking with his back
Legs and sometimes taking the brush from me.

Kitcat manages the brush
as best he can holding
the brush with his paws
moving his face over
the metal teeth.

He flips over exposing his furry
Belly knowing my irresistible
Urge compelling me with my fingertips
To touch his softness while he's alert his

Mouth is open ready to bite his eyes
Are excited expectant and I can't
Resist and grasp his face with a hand while
He swivels about with his spine kicking

With the nails of his back legs biting my
Hand as I'm spinning him about using
Both hands grabbing and slapping so quickly
He can't respond and seems a little stunned

Swiping with his — nail-less — front paws at my
Hands but more often than not he misses.

Grabbing and lifting slightly
Kitcat's haunches while he's
on his back excited
I seize control as he can't
bite swipe or kick.

Johnnie used to be more affectionate
But now he's skinny and thinking mostly
About eating yowling at me when I
Enter the home following me around

Even though he eats more than Kitcat does
Kitcat being twice the size of Johnnie
With Kitcat pouncing continuously
On Johnnie leaving tufts of hair on the

Floor though when I'm present I'll shoo Kitcat
Force Kitcat to release his grip stop him
From biting Johnnie about the neck make
Kitcat slink away while later I see

Both of them curling sleeping together
On a chair in blessed unconsciousness.

Old
skinny
hungry
bullied —
I'd sleep too
if I were Johnnie.

When I'm awake in the hours before dawn
I dwell on the hairline cracks that emerged
Within my family over the years
In a household empty of my children

And a spouse when I would much rather be
Sleeping but somehow I'm not managing
To turn my mind off — I've cleaned out the
Refrigerator but haven't gone through

The cupboards or decided which of the
Pots pans spices and utensils to keep
As dozens of items bespeak the love
My wife displayed in making our dinners —

There is the pot we used to brew our tea
And the knives that cut the chicken and fish.

Somehow our love
wasn't sufficient to
keep the family from
fracturing and wondering
why is painful.

Enso

Zen calligraphers make a circular
Motion with a brush creating in a
Swirl of ink and horsehair a symbol for
The way energy is manifesting

In the eddies of whirlpools and typhoons
In the cycling of daylight and night
In the repetition of the seasons
In the orbits of stars and galaxies

And even in the irresistible
Transitions from birth and exuberant
Youth to the maturation of middle
Age into the sober decline of death —

It's easier for me to believe death
Is a season in the cycles of life.

A crest of sunlight
is continuously
breaking upon the
earth revolving
about its axis.

I notice when a chickadee appears
In the bush beyond my window and it
Is hopping and darting its head about
Then suddenly it flits away — sometimes

I see a group of crows stabbing and
Tearing the carcass of a squirrel on
On the street — and they accommodate my
Passing car by flying away — I am

Aware of the persisting cold when snow
Is covering the ground and the roots of
The trees are embedded in frozen soil
In February and when seeing the

Bare branches and a blue sky I wonder
What would the gnawing of hunger be like?

Do the crows and
chickadees notice
a glorious open sky
while starving in
winter?

I'm looking for a woman with whom I
Could behave just like I do with Kitcat
When seeing Kitcat dozing in a chair
As I'm hoisting him in the air using

His shoulders as a grip gazing into
His eyes suspending his limpness turning
Him left and right hugging him to my chest
Getting his hair all over my shirt and

When returning Kitcat to his chair I
Pet him repetitiously rubbing him
One hand after another from his head
To his tail applying quite vigorous

Pressure and I know Kitcat enjoys it
Because he follows me asking for more.

Such exuberance
on a first date
is liable to
encounter
resistance.

I gained traction in my life after years
Of aimless effort by creating a
Sanctuary in the morning letting
My thoughts percolate listening to words

I heard yesterday attending to the
Emotion conveyed recognizing my
Grief and disappointment wallowing in
Sadness being critical and watching

Criticism dissipate considering
What to do repeating nonsense phrases
Enunciating ridiculous noise
Entertaining my cats shaving my face

Opening the curtains of the windows
Anticipating the sunlight later.

Problems need addressing
emotions are expressed
energy emerges
enthusiasm comes —
I don't know how.

I don't do anything without purpose
Even though I admit I often have
Nonsensical rationales like watching
Many murder investigations for

Self-improvement and the *dharma* says that
Sitting in meditation should be done
Apart from the lure of benefit — that
The epitome of refinement is —

Purposelessness — but really I must say
I practice Zen in the morning because
It quiets my thinking and provides my
Kinder and optimistic impulses

The liberation they need to blossom
Which generates such enthusiasm.

My joyful
nonsensical
exclamations
to my cats have
no purpose.

Every Saturday night there are dances
At the Tapestry Center where I can
Go instead of being alone and they
Know each other very well but also

Welcome newcomers and yes the moment
Came when lining up without a partner
When people looked away and I felt a
Pang but then a gentleman smiled and gave

Place when the fiddling began and we
Were swinging and exchanging partners some
With practiced skill and others not so much
Including me but the rhythmic touching

Holding smiling playing light-heartedly
Was worth the drive to Minneapolis.

Getting used to swinging
and consequent
dizziness is my goal.

So much effort is necessary to
Become a fiddler or a dancer
With a seed of desire serving as
Impetus to blossom into a dance

And I'd like to meet someone to talk with
Joining a light-hearted circle of friends
Indulging in such effervescent joy
Leaving behind a weight of memory

Eliminating apprehension in
A spontaneous celebration of
A kindly graceful motion of people
With the single men and women having

An opportunity to sample each
Other with a swing — could she be the one?

Maybe with
sufficient
swinging
practice
dizziness
goes away?

Apart from the company I had the
Most salient ingredient of the
Afternoon was the brilliantly blue sky
Reflecting off of the fresh fallen snow

With two wisps of clouds on the horizon
And the cold that made the rims of my ears
Much redder as the time passed as Hattie
Informed me in the course of our easy

Conversation as light as wispy clouds
Drifting in an open sky while she was
Pleased with the added stability
That a walking stick provided as we

Meandered on a trail in the prairie
Grassland of the Lake Elmo Park Reserve.

Her poodle Aries kept
putting a ball he was
gripping in his teeth in-
to my hand challenging
me to a tug of war.

I am better off than most of my age
Because I exercise and refrain from
Eating processed foods preferring apples
To potato chips so I'm flexible

And thin about my middle but the growth
Continues persistently regardless
Of my inattention as it's easy
To forget that underneath my socks my

Toenails do need trimming and it is hard
To be pompous scrunching over to the
Left and right twisting a toe getting an
Angle maneuvering the clipper for

A cut and managing my little toes
I can't be thinking about dignity.

I have a
crescendo
of difficulty
scrunching with
my left hand
trimming my left
little toe.

I am a curious mixture of waves
And particles responding with my eyes
And skin to the brilliant light of the sun
With instantaneous electrical

Impulses inside of my brain bringing
To life the drifts of snow outside of my
Window on a day of below zero
Cold that's hard to distinguish from any

Other morning when the sky is open
As the same pinpoint jewels of refracted
Light are visible in the resplendent
Banks of snow but on this morning birds are

Darting strenuously about doing
Whatever they can to keep from freezing.

Waves and particles
come to life and the spare
muscles bones and feathers
of birds endure the
cold and hunger.

My Dad managed sharp edged opinions for
Most of his life that he moderated
By playing Mozart or Shubert for an
Hour in the afternoon every day

On a grand piano and I could tell
Whatever fractious divisions were in
His mind were dissipated in a play
Of ethereal harmony and he

Did his best to pass on his essential
Love to my daughter through lessons and with
The gift of a studio piano
That's residing in my house because she

Hasn't a permanent home and perhaps
Music isn't her love of expression.

The piano is a
symbol of my
Dad's all
encompassing
enthusiasm.

The tiniest twig at the top of a
Cottonwood positions several leaves to
Catch waves of sunlight in summer and the
Whole tree absorbs a prodigious amount

Of radiation with wind stirring leaves
And light sparkling in leaves but in winter
Its branches and craggy bark are exposed
And for a moment the rising sun will

Paint the cottonwood a gorgeous orange
And then the shine fades the light diffuses
And it's revealed as a monstrosity
Of crooks and curves and twists and tangles as

An expression of nature without an
Inch of symmetrical beauty.

But clambering squirrels
and craggy cottonwood
bark are in harmony.

The lines of my property consist of
Right angles and my home is constructed
Of rectangles and triangles but when
I gaze about I see the apple trees

By my driveway with one producing red
The other yellow apples in fall and
Like the cottonwood on the corner by
The street their bare branches are a riot

Of directions apart from notions of
Symmetry surpassing any form of
Predicable pattern presenting me
With a vision of a voracious and

A savage appetite for sunlight that
With the tepid winter sun is absent.

The sight and scent
of apple blossoms
enticing the bees
is a bold display
of seduction.

I do believe that death is only a
Season of life and that a consciousness
Continues apart from memory and
Habit with minutest particles and

Distant galaxies playing their parts to
Spring into being this moment after
Another falling of snow leaving this
Morning the pinpoint sparkles of light in

The fresh snow that seeing somehow brings such
Peace and nourishment to me however
I'll be emoting later whatever
I'm able to believe with limited

Comprehension somehow something says to
Me there is no need to struggle so much.

The tiniest flakes
are falling straight
down here and there
and too tiny to be
snow.

Wisps of diffuse clouds are drifting at a
Lackadaisical pace this morning as
I am marveling at their feathery
Existence floating eastwards in a sky

Of a soothing shade of blue savoring
Their ethereal forms entertaining
Notions of destiny questioning
Whether it is really possible that

These clouds mingling with the sun and wind
Could ever become so smothering and
Weighty that they would have to disperse
And descend in the form of snow or rain

To become inexorably absorbed
In a current moving to the ocean.

Earth
air
fire
water
questions.

Sometimes a surprising inspiration
Comes to me giving me a gift of a
Glimpse of insight into the way things are
And I often smile with recognition

As an unarticulated hunch in
The form of a vaguely comprehended
And nagging but unaddressed conundrum
That was percolating underneath the

Conscious level of my awareness has
Finally resolved itself into a
Burst of clarity while I am walking
From one room and into another and

I will laugh with the joy of solving a
Dilemma I didn't know that I had.

Sometimes
on arriving at the
window I discover
that the inspiration
is forgotten.

Before we extended our knowledge we
Could endow the heavenly bodies with
Spirit and what a mystique the waxing
And waning moon would hold appearing so

Huge and orange on the horizon and
So distant and silver among the stars
While sometimes penetrating the morning
Or the afternoon beyond the clouds as

If to say remember the light of day
Is temporary and wouldn't we have
Savored the mystery of not knowing
How far away and how large it was but

Now we aim our radar at the moon and
Bounce our beams of careful calculation.

We know the earth is
a jewel of the cosmos
because we savor photos
of the earth taken
from the moon.

On occasion I doubt myself second
Guessing the quality of the choices
I make for instance when in connection
With other poets I notice they will

Compose a title for every poem
Providing a table of contents for
Easy reference and I have compared
My paucity of titles as a fault

But today I realized from day to
Day from quatrain to quatrain indeed there
Are breaks within the flow but really the
One hundred poems composing a book

For me signify the modulations
Of one joyously alive harmony.

So pick a page
any page and
see if something
communicates to you
of essential liveliness.

After he's partaken of the canned food
And also of the dry food that comes from
A bag Kitcat will jump onto the shelves
To a space that's next to a microwave

And he proceeds to caterwaul in his high
Pitched voice and he stares at me and will not
Be quiet which is how he behaves when
He wants to be fed which is a nuisance

Trick that he learned from Johnnie so I ask —
What do you want — and he looks me in the
Eyes because he's achieved a stature
Of height at eye level with me which is

Why I think he makes the effort to jump
There and insistently he inquires.

I use my fingertips
massaging the hair
between his ears and
inside his ears and he
shakes his head.

Upon arriving at my place of work
Which is the home where my mom is living
I enter through the garage and into
The printing room and see the printing press

That is a Ryobi press capable
Of printing 11 by 17
Or 8 ½ by 11 inch
Paper which are sizes my Dad and I

Used to print the journal that we published
Which I continue to publish after
Dad died and the Ryobi was rendered
Obsolete by the emergence of much

Better copiers so everyday I'm
Reminded of how the past is fleeting.

A running printing
press has a mechanical
and satisfying
rhythm that I
am missing.

I've concluded there comes a point within
Winter when exhaustion is established
After which the days become a dreary
Trudge to the horizon and I suggest

That February is a state of mind
Not necessarily corresponding
To the calendar as I have known a
Series of blizzards in March even in

April bearing down upon me as one
Continuous never-ending nadir
With no better name than February
Even as the shadowy wings of night

Are diminishing the light of day is
Strengthening if only in mockery.

Yet the sun shines in
February and at
the nadir the only
direction is better
eventually.

Dedicated to Mike Finley
King of the St. Paul Poets

We know the thousands and thousands of stars
Glimmering in the vast emptiness of
The night are accompanied by trillions
And trillions of stars that human eyes are

Incapable of seeing — we know that
Each photon of light lingers within a
Gaseous sphere for thousands and thousands of
Years before it discharges into space —

We know that the velocity of light
Is unsurpassable — and we know that
The pinprick points of light surrounding the
Earth have traveled billions and billions of

Years to penetrate a moment of our
Waking consciousness amidst our slumbers.

And yet each human
breath following breath
evinces a continuing
and precious
liveliness.

When I find myself awake a couple
Of hours before dawn with my thoughts cycling
Uselessly I have a choice to lie in
Bed exhausted or to put my cushions

Out and meditate so last night I sat
Determined to quell the cogitation
While Kitcat pounded on the door forcing
Me to rise and let him enter because

He wouldn't stop while Johnnie came to whine
At me because that is what he does while
Kitcat jumped from the bed scampering as
Fast as he could bolting out of the room

So I tossed Johnnie out and closed the door
When Kitcat pounced on him and Johnnie yowled.

Before dawn my
cats are watching
and waiting for
me to move.

Inside of a room cluttered with things that
Supported a printing process that is
Not ongoing — like a light table in the
Corner for laying out copy — I come

Everyday with a sense of gratitude
Because this room inside a house on the
Earth rolling on its axis around
The solar system and the Milky Way

Is here for me when the freshest light of
The ascending sun is entering through
The window and brightening the debris
Of life while I am sitting at my desk

Seizing morning clarity distilling
Experience and cavorting with words.

I have meandered
over several continents
consuming decades
unfocused dissatisfied
finally finding joy.

Breath continues breath blossoming inside
Of lungs and dispersing as a tonic
Throughout my body and inspiring
Me with clarity of mind once I've learned

The trick of attending to the lively
Process of breathing inhaling through my
Nose and releasing as a glorious
Relaxation peacefully quietly

Appreciating the sun and earth and
Leaves and oxygen and nitrogen and
Atmosphere even with the bare branches
Of February breath continues breath

And I don't have to focus attention
Or lift a finger to make it happen.

The simplicity
of breathing
is a gift.

On the verge of March
a thaw is biting drifts of
snow and water is
flowing across the streets down
to the current under ice.

— *Tekkan*

www.ingramcontent.com/pod-product-compliance
Lightning Source LLC
Chambersburg PA
CBHW042118100526
44587CB00025B/4103